A Matter of Dark Matter

A Matter of Dark Matter

Poems by

Kate Hutchinson

© 2022 Kate Hutchinson. All rights reserved.
This material may not be reproduced in any form, published,
reprinted, recorded, performed, broadcast,
rewritten or redistributed without
the explicit permission of Kate Hutchinson.
All such actions are strictly prohibited by law.

Cover by Shay Culligan
Cover art by Taneli Lahtinen on Unsplash
Author photo by Bourelle Photography

ISBN: 978-1-63980-106-0

Kelsay Books
502 South 1040 East, A-119
American Fork, Utah 84003
Kelsaybooks.com

*For all those who are working to bring
more light and love into the world*

Acknowledgments

I am very grateful to the editors of the following journals and websites for the previous publication of these poems, in their current or slightly altered forms:

3Elements Review: "The Anointing," "Expressway Mindfulness"
After Hours: A Journal of Chicago Writing and Art: "Singing in The Grocery Store on a Friday Night"
Awakenings Review: "Mild Depression" (as "Undiagnosed"), "After the Nervous Breakdown: A Haibun"
East on Central: "Cinderella on Stage" (as "Cinderella"), "Marcel Marceau Appears on My Birthday," "Gentle Yoga," "Labyrinth"
Gyroscope Review: "When the Water"
Hartskill Review: "Cold"
Haven: "Lifer"
Highland Park Poetry Muses' Gallery: "After Ice Skating," "For Elie Wiesel, 1928–2016," "Acclimation"
Illinois State Poetry Society: "Jettison"
Jet Fuel Review: "Rage Against Invisibility"
Minerva Rising: "Reading Faulkner with Teenagers"
A Quiet Courage: "Hunger"
Rat's Ass Review: "Heartthrob" "Pendulums"

A heartfelt thanks to the many family members and friends who have supported and encouraged me over the last 14–15 years as I've developed my poet's voice—my sister Jan Lundeberg, brothers Richard and Keith Hutchinson, and sisters-in-law Dana Hendrix and Tammy Powell; my Larkin Aunts JoAnn, Jeanie, Jenny, Judy, Joy, Jane, Janette and Uncle Jim; lifelong friends Tracey Repa, Paul Quinn, Lisa Mlodoch, and Melissa Moeller; dear teaching colleagues and mentors Peg Mangan, Robin Paul, Sandy Beguin, Jane Fraser, and Tom Herrmann; the many excellent poetry teachers whose classes I have attended, especially John Drury and Marilyn Taylor; and countless fellow writers with whom I have shared and discussed poems.

And always, love and gratitude for my parents—my father Bill, my biggest cheerleader, who passed away on August 17, 2021, just shy of his 90th birthday; and my mother Joyce, whose death at age 46 in 1983 first sent me to poetry in search of the right words.

Contents

I

Cold	15
Birds are Gathering: A Golden Shovel Poem	16
Solastalgia	17
When the Water	19
At the Altar of Bright Plastic Mounds	21
This Lowly Ground, 2020	22
Never Too Many Beans	23
Winter Solstice	25
A Matter of Dark Matter	26
Hunger	27

II

Fever Dream	31
Yesterday Is Illusion	32
Horatio's Exit	33
Bindings	35
All Wired Up	36
How Necessary It Is for One Body to Feed Another	38
Understanding Van Gogh and My Son	40
Reading Faulkner with Teenagers	41
Villanelle for the Voiceless	42
The Mowers	43

III

Listening to Gwendolyn Brooks	47
Around the World in Fourth Grade	48
Busse Woods, 1970	49

After Ice Skating	50
Lions Park Pool	51
The Anointing	52
Magazine Summer	54
Cinderella on Stage	55
Lifer	56
Sleight of Hand	57

IV

Losing the Last Parent	61
Your Hands	62
Awaiting the Diagnosis	63
Mild Depression	64
Agoraphobia	65
After the Nervous Breakdown: A Haibun	66
Marcel Marceau Appears on My Birthday	67
Rage against Invisibility	68
Heartthrob	69
Pendulums	70

V

Hand of God	73
Expressway Mindfulness	74
Jettison	75
Gentle Yoga	76
A Sonnet for Small Joys	78
For Elie Wiesel, 1928–2016	79
Labyrinth	80
Acclimation	82
Singing in the Grocery Store on a Friday Night	83
It All Matters: An Abecedarian of 2020	85

I

Cold

In the mass of browned leaves
packed into a crook of branches,
large and round as a classroom globe,
nestles a lone gray squirrel.

Who can say what's still hidden
when the trees shed their frills
down to hoop-skirt bones?

A hibernating heart beats so slowly
it barely warms the skin.
Even dreams cease in deepest snow.

Under the January moon
the wind stirs the nest's leaves,
ruffling the squirrel's ears and tail.
We must love something just enough.

Birds are Gathering: A Golden Shovel Poem*

*Here, transversal takes on a quality of communion,
the kind that arises when frontiers fall.*
                            —Jordan Kisner

                    Starlings gather on the patio. Here,
                    all has been muddied, the transversal
                    of resignation and want. Light takes on
                            the maudlin hue of a
                    reed-choked marsh, airless. What quality
                        abides when the sun dims? All of
                summer's gold wanes in my memory, communion
        a shriveled vine draping the fence. Over this darkening, a kind
                    of spiritual numbness settles in, a grayness that
                        dissolves desire. Still, the ghostly moon rises.
                    It is late, the blackbirds high in their roosts, when
                        a vole scurries across its last frontier.
                    I lie awake and listen for mountains to fall.

* The <u>last</u> words of each line in a golden shovel poem are words from a line found in another poem or text, used in order. The original line must be cited as an epigraph, as it is here. In this collection, all golden shovel poems are right-margin aligned.

Solastalgia

We measure our lives against
      the trees we grew up with
           their constancy
                continuity

We want them to tower above us
      gigantic, spiraling
           cathedral columns
                like Olympian shrines
           or Druidic sages

We want to see majestic elms
      like wings hovering over
           our children's schools
                and lining
           coastal avenues

Some of us still seek Appalachian chestnuts
            their precise locations
                kept secret
            like holy relics

      To find them is like sighting
            Bigfoot or the monster of Loch Ness
                People steal their bark and leaves
            as proof that they exist

      The ash trees are disappearing now –
            their once luxuriant crowns
                thinned to eerie
                      transparency
                            bared twigs against

ethereal blue

To be aware of our surroundings
    is to open ourselves
   to constant grief
        each tree in our memory
          a ghost
        each tree yet living
            haunting us with its
                aura of doom

      We have begun to name
          our favorite trees
              in a desperate plea
          to hold them here

      We have begun to know
          that the way of the world
              is to disappear

When the Water

After the hurricane we saw photos of people
lining highways with their boats, waiting.
They motored slowly into the flooded streets
like t-shirted gondoliers calling out to the silent
rooftops, an armada of eyes and ears.

There, an old couple in life vests held hands.
There, a dog straddled a tree branch, a mother
clutched her child atop a sofa, half-submerged.
Brown water swirled, then stilled, stubbornly
believing it belonged in dens and nurseries.

~ ~ ~

In Greenland some narwhal hunters
tell reporters that ice sheets were only
three inches thick this year, too fragile
for dog sleds. They fish now in kayaks
or hunt for walrus in berg-riddled fjords.

Amid echoes of calving from gray glaciers,
families in Qaanaaq share the meager catch
with dogs who stretch and whine with ennui.
Now, they say, they must rely on the kindness
of occasional outsiders. Or simply pray.

~ ~ ~

The people at this party get younger every year.
With wired ears and electronic palms
they signal each other in new languages,
clustering at the bar glowing green with neon,
their faces frozen in silent-movie laughter.

When it's clear that I have become invisible,
I escape the patio to find the pier, under lattices
of golden locust leaves, then step into a canoe.
I row to the center of the lake where all is still—
in my head a forgotten song. My son's face.

At the Altar of Bright Plastic Mounds

Our anti-Eden, this beach—
this post-post-Stonehenge—
this monstrosity of bottles, baubles and beads
the ocean gods coughed up and laid at our feet.

Nature has always been our mortal enemy,
claws and breath and fatal branches after dark.

Let this be our beach then. Let us wear
six-pack rings around our collective neck,
bottle caps fused into our backs like some freakish tattoo.

Nearly every stone, leaf, and breath of air
contains our heavy signature. Humans' legacy:
to possess, to ravage, to scar, or to neglect.

We leave behind a swath of savage footprints,
a hellscape of epic proportions.

Let us soon suffocate under the weight
of barges piled high with detritus—
our manifest destiny writ large in neon pink—
sinking, sinking, sinking.

This Lowly Ground, 2020

Borrowed time and borrowed world and borrowed eyes
with which to sorrow it.
                              —Cormac McCarthy, *The Road*

Within days of the asteroid blasting a hole on Earth,
most life on the planet withered, burned, and died.
The West holds graves of dinosaur bodies stacked side
upon side, where ten or more had gathered and starved.

Such graves exist for human beings as well,
though famine hasn't always been the cause—
pandemics, wars, and genocide have gnawed
across the globe, where ghosts linger to tell

of desperation, facing evil or pain
in those final hours, their only hope that peace
awaited them in death. I've learned through the years
that small joys and love are all we may attain.

I dare to dream of the life that lies ahead
while trucks are being filled with bodies of the dead.

Never Too Many Beans

The little-known economist warns us
in a magazine that it will get much worse.
You will have to give up a whole package
of toilet paper for one ripe tomato, she says.

Money will become worthless. Now
look around you. What will you part with
to get one pound of good coffee?
A handful of raisins to sweeten your bread?

It happens every eighty years, a well-known
historian says on TV. Once per lifetime,
a great suffering. Our grandparents told
of standing in line for government-issued

cheese and rice during the Great War,
coupons for every household. Some became
hoarders afterward, afraid they would never
have enough. My mother stashed cans of soup

for thirty years. After the war, they found
jewels hidden in apartment walls in Paris.
Even now, surely gold lies buried under trees
across Poland and Russia, owners long gone.

Which of us will be willing to make do
with one cup of sugar or a half-dozen eggs?
Which of us will find ways to take more,
lining the larder while a baby starves next door?

Today, basements fill up with bags of flour
and pinto beans, bottles of water. How much
salt will be enough to last an apocalypse?
What will be the first to disappear, potato chips

or cases of beer? What are you willing to lose?
For three juicy plums: your mother's pearls.
For a pound of ground beef: your rusting car.
For the last bar of chocolate in the world:

nothing anyone owns will be enough.
Nothing
will have to be enough.

Winter Solstice

Maybe it's alright that the
Christians stole the Solstice,
carried it off to church and
dressed it up with stars and crosses
and called the Son their own.

Those with ancient blood know
the wreaths and candles and songs
tell a different tale wherein
the promise of the Sun's rebirth
is powerful enough to bring hope,
and where Elder and Birch
are the wise men who share secrets
with the guardians in their
sacred woodland circles.

Once Earth's darkness told us
to be still and contemplate her
deep womb from which all
life springs; the ancient tombs
at Maeshowe and Newgrange
glowed with the first rays
of our reinvigored god as he
lit upon the buried cairns
promising life would come again.

So womb gave way to manger
and Earth's light to holy child, now
called the hope of all mankind. But
on the longest night under the black
dome of ice, Earth whispers still.

A Matter of Dark Matter

Dark matter is like an overflowing cup,
the present moment resting at the surface,
the great beyond bubbling up into supernovas.

Above the rim, time accelerates into
the mystery of the dark, overwhelming
the five percent that we can see and touch.

What lies out there, above the holy grail of time?
No one knows, though Einstein told us
it was not nothing. A matter of some consequence.

Darkness matters—a thought unsettling
to those of us who live in light. So how
reassuring to know dark matter is not full

of Massive Compact Halo Objects (MACHOs)
but Weakly Interacting Massive Particles (WIMPS)—
NASA's little joke spinning around us,

helping us believe no particle wars seem
imminent in space. Still, light years away
float the memories of collided galaxies,

one called—of course—Pandora's Cluster.
Here, tiny sparks still hurtle out into
the vast darkness, their fate unknown.

Hunger

—after Sharon Olds

I wanted to be there when the world ended

because I wanted to feel the earth cool—

not just oceans and rivers

but stars and even you—

it would be a hunger

to lie in an open field—

to take back perfection—

the beauty of the honeybee

in the eye of a daisy.

II

Fever Dream

Unmoored, marooned, the ship lurches.
I clutch the railing, momentarily stalled
in my quest to find the source of the smell—
glimmering onions and mushrooms, voluptuous
vegetables—sautéed by some magician below.
Three days after escaping brutal pirates, I
and two other survivors, starving, awaken
from dreaming about home, the sun peering
into the stifling cabin where we'd found refuge.
The savory incense pinches us, reels us in—
hypnotized, unguarded, naked with hope.
Whispering prayers, we make the descent
into the marrow of the iron beast,
where at last we discover great fires
popping with the brilliantine slick of oil.
Outlined by the blaze in the blackness
is a taut, tattooed chef, preening like some
La Scala diva and brandishing machetes
like Ginsu knives, his wry smile daring us
to step forward and eat . . . or be eaten.

Yesterday Is Illusion

Every memory becomes a lie
        merely by evaporating
drifting into the periphery
            quavering through concentric rings

There—and there—and there—
        and gone—shrapnel images
somersaulting into gray matter
            hundreds lost behind every blink

Billions of buffers against truth
        in this bacchanal of pixels
no aide-de-camp with definitive proof
            in a briefcase just outside the door

In kaleidoscopic arrangements
        on each reel of daily film
our own Rorschachs and Pollocks dance
            with an abandon we are powerless to thwart

We are not who we think we are
        photo collages pooling into identity
no plot line with a narrative arc
            we breathe and we dissolve

Horatio's Exit

Steadfast and true for five hundred years, he's had enough.
By Act Five, scene two, he'll be gone, before the swords fly.

Even for this good man, Hamlet's "heart of hearts,"
his soul's chosen one, it is finally too much to bear.

None of us would blame him. How taken for granted
is the loyal friend, left to clean up the spectacular mess

of the hero—and for what? Royal deaths are inevitable.
But always he remains, bereft. He has long dreamt

of a wife—a good woman, bonneted and fair, sewing
by the fire, then warming his bed. *Is it really true,*

she'd one day ask, *that in the end, you cradled his head
and offered him to the angels, kissing him goodnight?*

And he would say, ever humbly of course, *Yes, my love,
it was I who did these things and more. The most horrible*

*scenes I witnessed, there at Elsinore, year after year—
from ghosts to madness to piles of dead on the floor.*

He'd endure her pity, yet another burden. He'd not tell
how he tried to warn the prince of foul play, or how

he was asked to reveal all to the new, steely king.
He lacks the pride to take credit for that. Repelled

by power, he wishes only for peace and rest. And so
we must compel him to escape this endless loop, for we

must admit, in the end, he is unneeded. He has always
known this, too, which endears him to us all the more.

His very presence is a pale charade that such a man
exists at all. Now let him watch for the last time as

the ill-fated prince enters the hall to unsheathe his sword.
Horatio has turned his back on treachery, this chaotic end,

on all that is wrong with that miserable world.
Let him step into life, burnished, unburdened.

Bindings

Space crews float in zero gravity for a year,
    busy with upkeep and experiments,
eating rehydrated foods and working out
    with weighted boots to prevent
atrophy. In bed each night, they note their
    thoughts and feelings so NASA can learn
how their self-concepts change: do they
    still feel fully human—of earth and ashes?

    What of their relationships with friends
        and loved ones? Hurtling around Earth
    at 17,000 miles an hour, do they feel
        the waxing of love when nearing home
    or its waning when they're 8,000 miles away
        above foreign oceans? Is this coolness
    different than when we live across town
        but never find time to pick up the phone?

        When Scott Kelly was aboard, he grew two inches
            taller than his twin Mark. His chromosomes
        changed. Tethered to the station to make repairs,
            did he think of the cords of flesh that snaked
        between them in the womb? Perhaps that night
            he wrote of a loneliness strange and profound,
        a new kind of solitude. Of being no longer a clone
            but refashioned—part clay, part moon.

All Wired Up

> *None but those who have experienced them can conceive of the enticements of science.*
> —Dr. Victor Frankenstein in *Frankenstein,* by Mary Shelley

My physical therapist sticks the pads
to my lower back and abdomen,
stringing me like a Christmas tree,
then twirling me around so I can
lie down without tangling up. She
flicks the switch and cranks the dial
till I feel the tingles that are to
train my nerves to find new paths.
Sometimes it kind of seems to work.

~ ~ ~

When we were kids, our dad stuck
needles in Mom's arm 3 nights a week
as she sat in their bedroom chair
and watched her blood snaking
in tubes to the kidney machine. Dad
turned some knobs and watched meters
to avoid mishaps that could be fatal.
Hums and beeps were our lullaby for
13 years, till the illness finally took her.

~ ~ ~

One year in junior high art class,
our teacher helped us make marionettes
using papier mâché, pieces of wood,
and string. Six of us decided to create
the Brady Bunch kids—my little Cindy
complete with yellow yarn hair. Greg's
shirt stripes bled and Marcia's eyes
were crooked, but we staged a little show,
our fingers making the bodies flop about—
at age 12 already practicing playing God.

How Necessary It Is for One Body to Feed Another

The hummingbird's slender beak sips
    at the purple cup of weigela

        as if cradled by a gossamer net

    a thousand crusted krill swim
    into the mouth of the humpback whale

        unbidden, unmawed

I think of this because when you were small

    you didn't know you could reach
    for my hand to plead for more

        of what hadn't filled you

But this does not mean I do not think about

    the hummingbird and the whale
    which must tell me something

        about nourishment, about
        the thin threads we cannot see

All year the West has withered

      last night a mother coyote
      pawed at a nest of mice

            while a newt awoke to find
            a lone fly in the lakebed

And you, who lie awake with thoughts I will never know

      you have not yet seen the moonflower
      uncoil its white petals

            in the glow of silver night

Understanding Van Gogh and My Son

When his mind went wrong, he became all heart.
—Adam Gopnik

Who can understand the turmoil—when
suddenly nothing makes sense, when his
eyes and hands freeze in panic, when his mind
loops again and again over where he went
astray, the scrambled words, all wrong.
Please no, do not reject me, he
silently pleads. Love me. When he became
a man it got so much harder. All
he knows is the constant bruise of his heart.

Reading Faulkner with Teenagers

When we get to chapter seven
where the orphan Joe is whipped
by the man he now calls father,

trousers down in the gray barn,
kneeling over the scripture he
refuses to learn, my students

recoil, appalled—their sympathy
for this boy on the page as real
as if he knelt before them.

Shouldn't it be easy for me
to spot the likely one or two
among them who have felt

the sting of the belt, the touch
of a hand in soft and secret
places, or the lash of slurs

across a red-flushed cheek?
How is it that children—too
young to fathom the bitter

contracts of love or the dark
scope of its thirst—learn to mask
the deepest betrayals, the ones

inflicted in the very rooms
where meals are shared, where
they too were once told that

God would find them if only
they prayed hard enough?

Villanelle for the Voiceless

Their backpacks are heavy and weighing them down
as they file off the bus in the dim morning light
with problems too large for the shoulders they own.

How can they possibly sit and focus and learn
when their parents may be missing by bedtime tonight?
Such huge, heavy burdens keep weighing them down.

The chance of bloodline, of a face deemed too brown,
now threatens the home won through hard-earned fight.
Such betrayal will not fit on the shoulders they own.

As children they claimed their voices, found their ground,
and bloomed into youth who reach and dream and strive.
But those backpacks, so heavy, now weigh them back down.

These days they don't speak, since to make any sound
risks the arrival of uniformed men in the night.
But how should they shoulder such fear all alone?

Their eyes reveal an anxiety deeply profound.
They are starlets whose futures hang on *maybe* or *might*.
We must strip off the backpacks weighing them down
and settle them upon new shoulders—our own.

The Mowers

They pull in at 7 a.m. sharp on Thursday
as they have every week since April,
every summer for the last fifteen years.
The pick-up truck and trailer are nestled
at the curb, cones placed at the front
and back. Three men in orange shirts
and yellow vests unload the machines,
start the engines. Two mowers and
a trimmer wind around the circle of lawns
in the gathering summer heat. By nine
they're done, packed up and headed out.

These men, whose names I do not know,
may or may not be the same who came
last week, last year, or a decade ago.
Black-haired and brown-skinned, they tend
to our yards while we sleep or watch
from windows, sipping our cups of coffee.
Our homeowner's fees pay their wages,
these men who push mowers all summer,
drive plows in the cold, and likely take
odd jobs in between to make ends meet.

Some days I step out for the newspaper
and wave hello, exchanging smiles as they
pull their machines down the wooden ramp.
Self-conscious in my slippers, I wonder
what they think of my clothes or my car,
then remember I am as much of a nobody

to them as they are to me. We go about
our business. Our selves and our plans,
our losses and loves, remain shrouded
with the invisibility my privilege affords me
and the needs their families demand of them.

III

Listening to Gwendolyn Brooks

What an invitation she offered into her world of words,
where grandmothers' kitchens came alive with smells, where
brown girls feared harsh hands, where shady pool players
lurked and jazzed in smoky bars. Words cartwheeled and
        caromed

over my head—my words but somehow not my language—
sharper, prickly playful, red with anger and blue with tears.
They were gemstones I fondled in my coat pockets
and sang into new rhymes as I walked home from school.

As I grew, she shrank, Ms. Brooks. By her third visit, to my
college classroom, she was small as a child, orthopedic shoes
shuffling. Only then did I recognize the power in those
flashing eyes, the serrated edge of her tongue: warning us

about old, *jellied rules*. Daring herself to wear *brave stockings
of night-black lace*. Shaming those pink ladies of Glencoe
who love *the poor* but not *their stench*. Something like wisdom
seeded between my ribs, then—tendrils of a soul taking root.

Around the World in Fourth Grade

I never felt envy or jealousy, only
amazement as Lola raced up and down

the aisles, winning at multiplication
"Around the World" in math class.

That year we'd begun to practice
the building and breaking of alliances,

and snubbing with birthday party list
omissions, but Lola and I were glued.

Her joy was mine, unfiltered. When she
reached the final desk and answered first,

I cheered the loudest. Who are we
at nine or ten but bundles of eyes

and ears—alive, alert and raw, as yet
unbowed by the heavy slaps to come?

I marveled open-mouthed upon hearing
Neil Armstrong's voice from the moon,

felt ecstasy at the sight of Peggy Fleming
twirling in a blur on the ice, her hair

a nimbus flowing around her tilted head.
They showed me there's nothing above us

but bright, thin air—and that I alone
could decide how to breathe it all in.

Busse Woods, 1970

Winter Saturdays, we'd follow Dad down the path
lugging our skates, seeking the marsh that would now
be transformed into our own private ice rink.

My brother, too little to skate, shoveled ahead of us
as we wound around the perimeter between trees
and worked our way to the center, wary of cracking ice.

Twirling on one foot, I'd look up through crooked limbs
to see gray sky and my own puffs of breath. Dad told us
that long ago this land held thousands of native people,

mainly Sauk and Fox, who may have used these trails
and ponds in their daily lives. It was a thought
too hard for me to grasp as a child, that people

of another time could have been where we were now.
And within a few years, the forest would undergo
such change that all our spirits would be swept away –

Salt Creek dammed for a fishing lake, miles
of paved bike paths snaking through the woods,
and picnic areas bringing crowds year-round.

The footpaths are now only a memory, paved over
or hidden by foliage. We were the last to follow them,
in times when the woods still held wild places.

After Ice Skating

Muffled—the perfect word
for how sounds disappear
into bathroom air when our damp
outerwear hangs all about—
snow pants draped on the shower rod,
scarves, mittens, extra socks
and my long, tasseled stocking cap
crowding brackets of the towel rack
like a patchwork tapestry
knitted by some crazy aunt.
That smell of melted snow—
damp and earthy, mud and mist—
is childhood laid out to dry
while we sit on the little rug,
pink-cheeked and matty-haired,
rubbing life back into our toes—
white winter joy between us.

Lions Park Pool

My mind returns again to the pool,
that steadfast slab of aquamarine
filled each year for the village kids
who descended on bikes to bare their limbs
in a frenzy of seasonal freedom.

Sensory overload is what we craved—
(is this why I remember it so well?)
—twinned smells of chlorine and coconut,
the din of splash, shriek and whistle,
that blissful rush of cool on skin
newly crisped by the exulting sun.

One best friend was all you needed.
Layered between blue water and sky
afloat on our backs, or eeling through forests
of glowing legs, our eyes open and stinging—
we swam and dived till we pruned,
then scurried over concrete to flimsy towels
laid out along the chain-link fence.

Lying on our bellies, chins on arms,
we'd gaze at the bronzed lifeguards
with idolatry pure and unashamed. Our legs,
(so small and unshaven) splayed behind us
like knob-kneed foals', could jump up
on a whim to climb to the high dive and soar—
then touch bottom and catapult back into air.

Our nascent bodies, arms wide to life,
hang frozen in that moment—
where buoy ropes and Top-40 beats
reassure us—yes. This happiness is all
we'll ever need to claim or to believe in.

The Anointing

We must've been twelve that summer,
launching into life with every dive
off the pier. You chose me with a whisper
and out we crept at midnight, silent,
risking dreaded phone calls home but
knowing the counselors had drunk
illicit beer and slept like the dead.

I can still hear the chirping cicadas, feel
leaves tickle my ankles as we followed
the path to the dock. A haze had settled
over the lake, the moon a woolen effigy
of itself casting an eerie glow. We
dipped our feet in the cool water.
Our legs touched, one spot of warm.

Did we talk at all before the moment
we heard soft splashes and saw, in the
distance, a white figure rising to beckon us?
You called her the Lady of the Lake
and said she had made us the Queens
of the Forest. We were not at all afraid.
We held hands in our invincibility.

Upon waking in the cabin, I was sure
it had been a dream. Or had I been
sleepwalking? You were nowhere
to be found. But then, as we loaded
onto buses for home, you saw me from
your window and winked, touching
your head where your crown had been.

Why is it in waning memory your name
has slipped away? Did the two of us
really go to the water's edge that night
and see the white-robed figure, believe
we were anointed as mythic beings?
Or were you just an inner part of me
emerging, sword drawn, in the darkness?

Magazine Summer

There she is in the scrapbook:
the model in the photo from 1979,
still beautiful, smiling in her
azalea-pink sweater and white skirt,
hair in perfect swoops against
her cheeks and shoulders,
lavender pumps perched on the steps
of some antebellum façade.
She's a model selling clothes, but
to me she was quintessential—
backlit with sunlight, poised for
a life of confident elegance.

That year I regressed into
second girlhood and anorexia,
feeding only on the fear of a world
that I was sure would eat me alive.
All summer, preparing to leave
for college, I lay on my bed among
the glossy pages of *Glamour, Redbook,*
and *House Beautiful,* dreaming a future
of warm comfort and perfection—
flower-filled parlors with pastelled walls,
billowing draperies, cats coiled on divans.
From closets of skirts and sweaters
and ribboned straw hats, I could one day
emerge as the girl from Ipanema,
carefree and gazed upon,
a photograph glued to a page.

Cinderella on Stage

Somewhere in the third week
   it dawns on her. She spins and spins,
broom in hand, then dips and races
   as she cleans her evil stepmother's
kitchen floor, all to the frantic pace
   of the orchestra, her lace tutu smudged
to look tattered, charcoal brushed onto
   her perfect face. *So how is my life
any different?* she suddenly thinks.
   Half-starved and spent, day after day,
valued in the end only for her beauty
   and graceful turn of leg. Beaming
on Prince Charming's arm during
   curtain call, she sees the front row full
of little girls, eyes agleam, mothers
   like sentries between them. A worm
writhes inside of her. All this pink
   you see is mere fluff, she wants
to tell them. My crown, these eyelashes,
   are fake. What is real: my gnarling feet.
The constant dream of cheeseburgers
   and chocolate shakes, of whole days
spent in bed or on the warm shore
   of a teal-blue lake. Cinderella gets
her prince. I'll be back on this stage
   tomorrow to spin with my broom
again and again until my body breaks.

Lifer

Years later, fear lingered in dreams:
obscene rolls of fat at my waist,
jeans popping apart at the seams,
hogs for thighs, puffed doughy face.

The old haze of humiliation
vaporized (I thought) at twenty
still lingered, the memory cased in
every cell. Thirty years later, my slight

frame seemed at times illusory—
the chubby girl still hidden inside
waiting to re-emerge, huge Hershey
bar in hand, bagel smeared with butter.

I walked the thin sugared line between
control and chaos, warning myself
that each pound may lead to obesity.
Vanity, thy name is size two, else

why the struggle? Now gray-haired,
face lined by years, I have no reason
to care, but some nights at the mirror
I still search curve and flesh for flaws.

Sleight of Hand

The therapist tells me I can fool myself,
play a trick on my own mind, like a magician
making the Ace of Spades disappear
or producing a bouquet of roses out of thin air.

He taps his wand and I enter 1969,
small living room aglow with Christmas lights.
There I am, curled up on the couch,
its pattern worn thin on the oversized arms.

Knees to my chest, I am trying to be small.
My brothers, sister and father sit around me
and we eat donuts, drink eggnog,
our usual rituals. Without Mom, nothing works.

Tomorrow we'll dress up and visit her,
the hospital staff indulging us with a party room—
tablecloth, turkey, Kool-aid and cake,
Mom wheeled down in her pink robe and yellow skin.

Now, looking back, I remember only fear.
I see my glassy eyes, the way they stare
at the tree, tuning out my brothers' horseplay
and Julie Andrews' caroling on the console.

At once both nine and thirty-nine,
I walk toward myself and sit down gently,
then place my grown-up hand on my own
small cheek, eyes wet, throat tight.

I've come to tell you it's going to be alright,
I say. I look up into my own face, see the years
worn into lines. My arms reach out
and I am contained, both mother and child.

Moments later, as with the swish of a cape,
I return to the doctor's chair, arms at my sides,
drained and warm. I will go back again:
to the girl of twelve with her fickle friends,

to the preyed-upon fifteen-year-old,
the lost anorexic at nineteen, the nervous
co-ed hiding in her boyfriend's shadow,
the bride waking with regret on her honeymoon.

Each rabbit placed into the hat becomes
another dove emerging from a silk scarf,
until I feel that I am finally whole—
sawed-in-half woman stepping out of the box.

IV

Losing the Last Parent

Siblings reach out
across mountaintops
to clasp hands.

How vast the sky becomes
when no one is here
to rein it all in for us
and clamp it down
at the edges.

Your Hands

Open your hands if you want to be held.
—Rumi

After your children are asleep, you open
a window to breathe deep the lilac air. Your
chin resting on your up-cupped hands,
you gaze into the moonlit yard and wonder: If
you woke tomorrow as your teenage self, would you
choose all this again? Would you want,
still, the American narrative—to
marry, to mother, to live in this house, to be
hands for others—if you knew what your future held?

Awaiting the Diagnosis

To live in the place of not knowing
requires a delicate high wire dance,
both necessary and wholly unnerving.

Dip one toe down to the center ring
and you're trapped in a gloom-and-doom trance.
So stay in that place of not knowing.

Lean the other way, and you're overflowing
with false security, an entitled *bonne chance*.
It's necessary—though downright unnerving—

to hang centered on that wire, wobbling
and alert, prepared for either circumstance,
living fully in the place of not knowing.

Allow a touch of doubt, a spark of hope, yoyo-ing
on a tight leash in your step-by-step advance,
balanced in that place of not knowing.

When you finally learn where your path is going,
you'll land squarely, without a backward glance,
since you labored so hard at not knowing.
Now—finally—calm. Your heartbeat slowing.

Mild Depression

A little seed. Nestled deep somewhere
behind my left ear. Some mornings—
winter usually, glum and gray—it wakes
with a whimper. Nudged by a dream
perhaps—one of those with a bleak
landscape and a lonely wind, or
an abandoned child, wide eyes pleading.
Or my mother alive again, though always
in dreams I am aware she has been
long away. To look upon her only
brings an ache. Opening its tiny eyes,
the seed cowers, mourning for the world.
And as I wake, I feel its tears flow
into my veins. Some days, the deeps
of my bones never stop weeping.

Agoraphobia

Not till we are lost can we hope to be found.
—Henry David Thoreau

It happens when I'm alone—driving—suddenly not
aware of where I am, who I am, panicked—till
I see the pharmacy, the street sign.   Remember.   I
do this again and again, wooed by inner apparitions. I am
afloat like orbiting astronauts who say they feel lost
each time the sun disappears, when they can
no longer orient by north or south. How do I
let go of phantoms in fog? How is it I hope
that a traffic light's sudden red dot will pull me back to
myself? I yearn to be what I cannot be:
more than phosphorescence.   Found.

After the Nervous Breakdown: A Haibun

June: summer break, the enormity of an entire day. Still raw
from the impact—the bruise of brain scuttle and shock—
only recently able to let my mind wander without reeling—
the need for calm draws me into sunlight, the safety of
bugs and birds who never question how to be. I emerge
freshly washed, walk the path to the pond, grass so
unbearably green. I remove my shoes and let each toe
feel the damp grass, finger tender blades, fused to earth.
Tiny ripples spread across the pond from a pair of
mallards bobbing at the far shore. Birdsong warbles
in the air—robins, finches, shrill redwing blackbirds.
Eyes closed, slow breaths, I feel the air warming
into summer. I lie back gently and count to ten. At first
a slow levitation, rising above the pond, then speeding,
the pond becomes a small oval, houses tiny rectangles,
the air in my lungs light and cool, higher still to see
miles and miles of green fields and gray strings of roads,
high enough finally to see the rounded edges of Earth.
I float there. Beholden to no one. Smiling into the ether.

>   from the distant stars
>   the earth is an azure whirl
>   and I, miniscule

Marcel Marceau Appears on My Birthday

Marcel Marceau stands on my front porch,
hands behind his back. He smiles, making
the daisy tattoo under his left eye crinkle.

I ask him in, but he shakes his head no. He shrugs
and peers over his shoulder, raising his eyebrow,
beckoning me to guess what he is holding.

What is it, I ask myself, that I have been wanting?
What is it that only a mime could bring? I'm stumped.
Is it a rabbit in a hat? He looks sad, shakes his head.

Wild guesses are all I can offer. *A striped shirt
and beret?* He silently laughs, mouth open,
shoulders pumping up and down. This could take

all day. *Will you give me a hint?* Then he puckers
his lips as if to blow me a kiss. And so I know.
Marcel Marceau brings his hands from behind

his back, holding them open so I can see they are
empty. He crosses his hands over his heart and bows.
I bow deeply in return. When I look up, he is gone.

Rage against Invisibility

*Your ability to see is sometimes only as good as
your willingness to go unseen.*
—Meghan Daum, *The Unspeakable*

Not quite into your
dotage, you retain the occasional ability
to make others believe you exist—to
appear as more than vapor. Most see
just a woman, generic as porridge, who is
on the cusp of crepe paper. Sometimes,
you admit, a second cardigan is the only
refuge on this breezy verandah as
your curfew fizzles. Pure oxygen is as good as
sex or Jazzercize in the afternoon anymore. Your
leopard-print Fridays long gone, only a willingness
to attempt yet another waltz across the terrazzo, to
maintain your legendary ginger tongue, to not go
gently into that good nightclub, will keep you from being unseen.

Heartthrob

Oh, gorgeous, of course the demons
found you on the road less traveled.
The clichés of gig life have followed you
to this bar where a bad hip and bad credit
outpace your backbeats and rim shots.
Your beret, backward with a too-cool tilt,
no longer rests upon Dionysian curls
or adds a jaunt to your wink. Aged beyond
your peers, you lean against the wall
and try to count the days, joints, beers
or blues since the last time nothing hurt.
You learned long ago there's no
salvation in placing blame. Now,
atonement comes just four nights a week,
on the worn-out stool behind the drum set,
the battered heads thinned, transparent
as you are. Now, there is only sleep
or numbness—and the thrashing beat that
pulsates through the crowd and repeats,
a hundred hearts pumping life into yours.

Pendulums

The new atomic clock will take 14 billion years
to gain or lose one second, using oscillations of atoms
as a pendulum. I think of a tiny swing set in a teardrop.

This clock can also be used to detect dark matter,
I've been reading, but this seems strange to me
since it means finding what can't be seen.

We took 13 years to decide we couldn't live together,
but gravity keeps us near enough that we may collide.
Each morning I see the sun drift farther north, until

it's too heavy to lift itself over the horizon by the time
I arrive at work. I sit in the half-dark watching snowflakes
on the windshield forming random designs, and I think

of the time we stayed out late by the campfire
watching ashes swirl into the night. We said one day
we would learn all the constellations, which barely change.

One day they might name all the stars. Out in space,
humans are tiny specks whirling in capsules
that could soon alight on the surface of Mars.

When I return home after work the house is dark.
I have to feel along the wall to turn on the light.
Some nights it takes a whole hour just to go up the stairs.

V

Hand of God

Another angel wafted as a cloud
over Texas last week, gown flowing
and wings outstretched. (Though to some,
her hairdo seemed more Princess Leia.)

The palette of the Creator is vast—
rain stains the concrete under a bridge
as the shroud of the Virgin Mary, while
Jesus appears in tree trunks and potatoes.

When I bought a red car to be safe,
was it the hand of God reaching down
to make two red cars crash in front of me
as I drove boldly from the dealership?

The Holy Spirit is indeed mysterious.
Like a drunk uncle, he teases and cajoles:
See me now? Yoo hoo—see me now?
He sticks out his tongue to make us believe.

Expressway Mindfulness

Tuesday. Not even mid-week
and already I'm spent, suffering
the accordion stop-go of rush hour,
needing to scrape from my skin
the film of ill-will settled over this
gray-black sea of commuters who
all see each other as equals in villainy—
keeping them from that glass of wine
waiting on the counter at home.

What's to savor in these non-moment
moments we are supposed to live fully in?
How deep into this compost heap
must I dig to find the fuse, then focus
and re-light it? In my bubble of steel
and polyurethane, I make a desperate
plea to Siri: *Play me the music of waterfalls,
of meadowlarks, of Aeolian harps.
Find—somewhere—the sound of bliss.*

Jettison

A writer friend faces this conundrum:
at 68, how many staples does he need?
His lifelong yen for office supplies has wrought
drawers full, but after some calculations,
he realizes thousands will be left unused
to molder or rust in someone's garage.

Another laments this brittle truth:
no one will want the paraphernalia
billowing around her, sparking daily joy.
Even her children scoff at her shoebox
of tattered wedding mementos, destined
for the landfill, that lonely lagoon of ruin.

What of my own accumulation? Boxes
of bird ornaments, ten bulging scrapbooks,
costume jewelry my mother once wore.
Enough books to light a bonfire seen
for miles. If I disappear tomorrow,
whose bulldozer will plow it all away?

To approach our waning years is to decide
when something's usefulness outweighs
its sentiment or pure delight. How will we know
when it's time to part with the beads and baubles,
to strip down to seashell white, empty shelves,
a clear mind, and a simple mat on the floor?

Gentle Yoga

Downward Dog, Lotus, Arching Cat.
    We breathe, stretch, breathe again,

holding as still as we can, trying
    to clear our minds, becoming either
more ourselves or something else.

Weakened and wobble-jointed,
    I struggle to stand firmly on one leg

to be a tree. Branches up, left foot
    against right calf, I quiver like an aspen
and can't defy my two-legged humanity.

Years ago, stuck in our grief,
    Dad and I attended a yoga class

on Sunday evenings. It was strange to be
    just the two of us. We became
curled nautiluses embracing our knees.

Now Dad can't remember our time
    in the gym, can only imagine his body

stretched as a seal or bending to his toes.
    He struggles to stand, leans on his walker,
complains he's awakened yet another day.

The trees outside have begun to leaf.
    To be so deeply rooted in one place

is to be other than human. Our arms
    and legs are made to move
across the earth, toward each other.

A Sonnet for Small Joys

Let me have small joys if it will
guarantee small pain: a goldfinch
in the hedgerow, a chocolate drop
on my tongue, just enough in the bank.
No dazzling flash of sunlight, please.
No best-selling book, no near-death climb
to an Alpine peak or swashbuckling kiss
on the deck of a cruise ship at dusk.
Let my last day on the job end quietly,
a few moments to clean out my desk.
Spare me Mr. Holland's opus, the crowd
applauding wildly in the auditorium.
And in the end, a garden in the warm dark
where I may cast off my pearls, one by one.

For Elie Wiesel, 1928–2016

Hope inspires the good to reveal itself.
—Emily Dickinson

                    Some have begun to say that hope
is a trap, that its rosy glow inspires
false faith. But when we stand in the
abyss, its dark chill creeping, no good
sunlit gardens to hoist ourselves in to,
we can only believe the last inner wick will reveal
its white nub, will catch and sputter, will ignite itself.

Labyrinth

Thick fog filters the morning light,
   obscuring the new-leafed maple out back.
Even a second cup of coffee can't bring clarity
   to what I should worry most about. I drift

   back to the jigsaw on the table where
      each piece has its place in the scene:
oak tree, butterfly, field of white daisies.
     In the dimness, no pieces seem to fit.

We are told that in their labs, scientists work
   all night to puzzle out the virus's secrets,
perhaps soon to discover a hidden message
   or a perfect algebraic equation.

   Again I am called to the wooded path,
     looping around the pond in an easy rhythm.
   Planes are still absent in the skies overhead.
     I keep walking as the fog lifts. Sunlight bathes

the grass, and sparrows twitter in the trees.
   I have read that the Buddha once gave
a silent sermon, where he mused upon
   a single flower in his outstretched hand—

      the hand, the flower, the awesome mysteries
    of airways and blood, filaments and nectar,
complexities evolved from ages ago and
   still as fragile in an unpredictable world.

Ripples in the pond lap at the shore.
    I walk on. Two chickadees begin their
call-and-response in the trees high above,
    using a language only they can know.

Acclimation

In the beginning, we crept out stealthily
for food, wide-eyed with fear that
the virus lurked on every box and bag,
silently questioning others' hands.
Our dreams flowed with goblins,
red-spiked and menacing in the dark.

By August we've trained up like puppies—
masks dangling from rearview mirrors
and Purell in the glove box. We follow
red dots and arrows on the floor, give
eye-smiles to eyes behind Plexiglass.
In our dreams only far horizons, shimmering.

Singing in the Grocery Store on a Friday Night

It starts when I'm headed down the baking aisle—
that unmistakable jazz riff with the finger snaps.

It's late—the dim, cavernous store nearly empty
and I'm bone-tired from the grind. Clapton's

notes fan the little flame on low inside me
and suddenly I'm leaning onto the cart handle

so I can hip-sway as I pass the cured meats
and cheese sticks, yogurt and eggs. I'm humming

along, *If I could reach the stars,* turning to seek
the coffee for the jolt I'll need in the morning,

when suddenly my filter's gone and I sing—
I would be the sunlight in your universe.

No one's near to hear me, and I wander
into the pet food aisle for no reason, those

bright pink and orange bags of Iams pellets
gleaming—*Baby, if I could, cha-a-ange*—then

shifting an octave higher for the low notes—
the world. All I need now is laundry soap,

but I linger near the Solo cups till the final
guitar notes, feel them reverberate down

to my toes. To think I almost didn't come.
Now, no need for a Saturday morning

venture into the cold. The song still in
my ears, I greet the pony-tailed cashier

who hides a yawn behind her hands. *Just
you and me and Eric Clapton,* I whisper

and smile, placing apples on the belt—
so ludicrously round and red and sweet.

It All Matters: An Abecedarian of 2020

Antiseptics. Air for our lungs and air hugs for our hearts.
Boxes of beans plus blue skies and bikes and bare feet.
Clorox on the shelf along with cat food, chocolates and coffee.
Doctors, yes, and drive-thru windows and drive-by birthdays.
Exercise, elastic waistbands, evergreens draped in the yard.
Facts and falsehoods on Facebook. Food kitchens.
Gloves and newly-gray hair and grandparents on screens.
Hospitals full of heroes plus houseplants and hummingbirds.
IV drips, igloos outside restaurants. Vivid imaginations.
Jeans, jammies, jigsaws, *Jeopardy!* and Jupiter kissing Saturn.
Keeping our distance but keeping the faith. Kindness.
Libraries, leaves greening then falling on lawns. Love.
Masks and music and movies and mothers and miracles.
Nurses, oh yes. Newspapers and neighbors on the front porch.
Oximeters, ovens full of bread. Open minds, open hearts.
Personal protective equipment. Pets on laps and leashes. Poetry.
Q-tip swabs and questions on quarantining.
Remdesivir plus reading, reading, reading.
Steroids, sourdough starter, and solos on balconies.
Toilet paper hoarding and TV. Treadmills. Tireless teachers.
Ultraviolet light and unsung unselfishness everywhere.
Ventilators. Vaccines! Vegetables from our own gardens.
Windows kept open and long walks and wine.
X-rays of lungs, experts who temper our expectations.
Yeast and yarn and yoga and yearning for normal.
Zoom gluing us together under zillions of stars.

Notes

"Birds are Gathering." Source of quote: "Thin Places," *n + 1 Magazine,* Spring 2015. The golden shovel is a poetic form created by Terrance Hayes in 2010 in honor of poet Gwendolyn Brooks.

"Solastalgia." This word is defined as "the emotional distress felt when one's home landscapes become unrecognizable through environmental changes." Some phrases in this poem were taken from Helen MacDonald in her essay, "Dead Forests and Living Memories," *New York Times Magazine,* 9/17/15.

"At the Altar of Bright Plastic Mounds." This poem was inspired by Nathaniel Rich's article, "Climate Change and the Savage Human Future," *New York Times Magazine,* 11/18/18.

"Winter Solstice." For a lovely audio version of this poem performed by writer and presentation coach Paul Quinn, visit my web page, *Life from Both Sides of the Window,* 12/20/20 post, "Reflections on Longest Night."

"A Matter of Dark Matter." Some details in this poem come from the website *NASA.gov.*

"Bindings." Some details in this poem come from the 2017 PBS/TIME documentary, *A Year in Space.*

"Understanding Van Gogh and My Son." Source of quote: "Van Gogh's Ear," *The New Yorker,* 12/28/09.

"Reading Faulkner with Teenagers." Joe Christmas, an orphan of unknown parentage, is one of the protagonists in William Faulkner's 1932 novel, *Light in August.*

"Agoraphobia." The original quote by Thoreau in *Walden* reads, "Not until we are lost do we begin to understand ourselves." It has been paraphrased in many forms over the years.

"After the Nervous Breakdown." A haibun is the combination of two poems: a prose poem and haiku. The form was popularized by the 17th century Japanese poet Matsuo Basho.

About the Author

Kate Hutchinson's poems and personal essays have appeared in over sixty publications and earned numerous awards, including two Pushcart Prize nominations. She has two previous books of poetry, *The Gray Limbo of Perhaps* (Finishing Line Press, 2012) and *Map Making: Poems of Land and Identity* (THEAQ Press, 2015*)*. Kate is active with local writing groups and state-wide poetry organizations, currently serving on the board of the Chicagoland Poets & Patrons where she chairs two annual poetry contests.

Kate leads workshops for poets of all ages, and she has served as a judge for a variety of writing contests. Over the last three years, she spent many hours working with Dr. Charles Smith, Chicago pianist and music savant, in editing his memoir, *The 88 Keys That Opened Doors,* available on Amazon. This year, she begins a new adventure as assistant editor for *East on Central*, a literary arts journal based in Highland Park, Illinois.

Outside her work as a writer and editor, Kate is a primary caregiver and guardian for her adult son, Ramon, who has autism. She retired in 2018 after 34 years of teaching English and Speech at a large high school in Chicago's northwest suburbs, and for many years she also served as her school's Fine and Performing Arts Coordinator. Kate is currently on the board of the Friends of the Library organization in her community, facilitating used book donations and sales that fund library programs. In her free time, she enjoys reading, taking walks among the trees, birdwatching, and solving the daily *New York Times* and *Chicago Tribune* crossword puzzles.

Find more of her writing here:
poetkatehutchinson.wordpress.com

www.ingramcontent.com/pod-product-compliance
Lightning Source LLC
Chambersburg PA
CBHW070550090426
42735CB00013B/3130